Towards an AI-Infused Revolution in K12 Education

AI in K-12 Education

Adam Smith

Published by A. Smith Media, 2023.

TOWARDS AN AI-INFUSED REVOLUTION IN K12 EDUCATION

First edition. May 30, 2023.

ISBN: 979-8223865780

Written by Adam Smith.

Also by Adam Smith

AI in K-12 Education

Intelligent Machines in the Classroom: Unlocking the Potential of AI in K12 Education

Making Sense of AI in K12 Education: A Guide for Teachers, Administrators, and Parents

The Future of Learning: Artificial Intelligence in K12 Education

Towards an AI-Infused Revolution in K12 Education

Unleashing AI in the Classroom: Strategies for Implementing Intelligent Technologies in K-12 Education

Unleashing the Potential of Artificial Intelligence in K-12 Education: Reimagining How Learning Happens

Breaking Down Bad Habits

Breaking Down Bad Habits: How to Overcome Self-Defeating Behaviors and Achieve Success

Standalone

Brain Dead: When It Comes To Improving Mental Health, What The Hell Are We Waiting For?

40 Things Intelligent People Do Daily

The Beginner's Guide to Quantum Computing & Mechanics
Open Source AI

Watch for more at https://books2read.com/adamsmith.

Table of Contents

Chapter 1: "Unlocking Potential: Using AI to Create a More Personalized Learning Experience for K-12 Students"

Advances in technology are opening up new possibilities for how we approach education, and more and more educators are turning to artificial intelligence to provide a more personalized learning experience for K-12 students. AI can be used to analyze student data and help inform instructional decision-making, to create an environment where each student can reach their full potential.

The potential of AI-based learning systems lies in the ability to provide more personalized instruction to students. AI systems can identify individual student strengths and weaknesses, recognize patterns in student behavior, and make suggestions for tailored instruction based on these observations. For example, a machine learning algorithm could be used to detect discrepancies between a student's performance in one subject and their performance in a further, thus pinpointing areas of instruction that could be improved. AI-based applications can also be used to identify which students are most likely to need additional help and suggest techniques for providing that help.

AI can also enable teachers to automate certain tasks. For example, AI can be used to grade multiple-choice tests, eliminating the need for a teacher to grade each question manually. Similarly, AI can analyze textbook content and generate a "smart search," suggesting related content for further investigation. AI can also be used in the admissions and enrollment process, automating certain administrative tasks to free up time for teachers.

AI-based personalized learning systems can also provide real-time feedback and recommendations to students to enhance their understanding of course material. For example, these systems can provide instant feedback on student work, which can aid self-reflection and the identification of areas for improvement. AI-based chatbots can also be used to provide students with engaging lessons and tasks, whilst AI-powered virtual tutors can 'step in' to help to understand challenging topics.

In addition to AI-based personalized learning, the use of virtual and augmented reality can also help to create a more engaging learning environment for K-12 students. By using 3D simulations or augmented content, students can engage with course material in more immersive and creative ways. For example, virtual field trips can expose students to various unique experiences which would be impossible to observe in a physical classroom.

AI-based personalized learning also offers a range of benefits to parents and educators. For example, AI can be used to automatically generate reports on student progress based on data collected from AI-powered systems. These reports can be used to gain insight into student performance and identify areas where instruction may need to be modified.

AI can provide a wealth of opportunities for K-12 students, parents, and educators. By utilizing AI-based personalized learning systems, teachers can create a unique learning experience for each student, enabling them to achieve their full potential. AI can also support the creation of virtual and augmented reality lessons, helping to create a more engaging and creative learning environment for students. The adoption of AI in K-12 education has the potential to revolutionize the way we learn, helping to ensure that each student can achieve their aspirations.

Chapter 2: "Leveraging AI to Create Customized Learning Experiences for K-12 Students"

Nowadays, artificial intelligence (AI) is used in a myriad of ways across several industries. Education, in particular, is one such area in which AI has been instrumental, mainly in producing customized learning experiences for K-12 students. Specifically, AI can be used to personalize content to students' individual needs and provide recommendations based on their learning trends. Additionally, AI-based tools can help teach students problem-solving and higher-order cognitive skills.

When it comes to customizing learning experiences, AI can provide teachers with insights into students' characteristics and learning preferences. AI-based algorithms can analyze learners' previous responses to help target content suitable to their level of understanding. This tailored learning experience can help lessen the cognitive load on students and encourages independent study. Additionally, AI can be used to provide assessment data and feedback on learning assessment progress, leading to better learning outcomes.

AI can also recommend relevant and engaging content to challenge learners. This can be through personal learning paths or interactive activities and games. AI-based tools can measure students' interest in certain topics and use that data to deliver content and activities that match the student's interests. This can also be used to predict learning outcomes more accurately.

AI tools can also play a role in enhancing the teaching process in the classroom. AI-powered chatbots can answer simple student inquiries and help provide self-directed learning opportunities. Intelligent tutoring systems can provide learning content that can be quickly customized as per the teacher's need. They can also measure the effectiveness of the teaching process in real-time and prompt the teacher to modify their approach accordingly.

AI-based technologies can incorporate adaptive learning algorithms to adjust the course of learning as per students' performance. Adaptive tutoring systems can measure students' performances and suggest learning paths based on the assessment results. This can help improve students' engagement levels and make learning more fun.

AI can also help to facilitate collaboration among students. It can suggest activities that can help build critical thinking skills. AI can involve students in meaningful discussions and facilitate peer learning. It can also provide recommendations about other relevant or related topics that students can explore.

AI can be of great benefit to K-12 students by tailoring their education experience based on their individual needs and preferences. This can lead to better learning outcomes and help teachers to focus on specific learning objectives. AI-based tools can make learning more engaging and help make the teaching process more efficient and effective. AI can also help to facilitate collaboration among students, leading to better learning outcomes.

Chapter 3: "Unlocking a Customized Learning Experience with Artificial Intelligence"

In recent years, Artificial intelligence (AI) has become an increasingly vital part of our everyday lives, in a vast range of sectors, from health and finance to retail and education. Within the education sector, AI is being used to create a customized, tailored learning experience for students through increased personalization, automation and analytics. At its core, AI aims to make the teacher-student relationship more efficient while enhancing the understanding of course material.

AI offers a variety of capabilities and services that can be used to create personalized learning experiences. According to Gartner Research, AI-driven technologies in education are typically leveraged "in areas such as keyword recognition, concept tagging, natural language processing, video-based learning, virtual tutoring and deep learning." These technologies can provide students with personal, specific instruction that allows them to work at their own pace, so that they can truly maximize their learning potential. With AI, students can receive an instruction tailored to their individual learning requirements, and teachers can make lessons that cater to the specific needs of each student.

At the same time, AI can automate and simplify many of the mundane tasks associated with learning, freeing up teachers to focus on other important tasks such as engaging with their students and preparing for upcoming classes. AI can be used to facilitate homework and project completion and recommendations could be automatically generated to help learners select the best content to help reinforce their understanding of the material. AI can also help teachers keep track of student progress and alert them to potential signs of struggle. These automated services, combined with human expertise, can lead to a more efficient learning process and promote increased student engagement.

AI technologies can be used to analyze student data better and generate detailed reports and suggested tasks that enable them to understand their progress and adjust accordingly. By tracking student commitments and habits, AI systems can help create a deeper understanding of each student's success rate, enabling teachers to create a bespoke curriculum that caters to their specific needs. AI can also be used to assess and evaluate student performance, allowing for personalized evaluations that go beyond the traditional grading system.

These AI-driven technologies facilitate an enriched and customized learning experience for students while also freeing up teachers' time so that they can concentrate on other important tasks. By blending the powerful capabilities of AI with real human expertise, educators can reap the benefits of a richer learning experience while also enhancing the teacher-student relationship. AI has the potential to revolutionize the way we teach and learn, and it's already being put to use in educational contexts around the world. As more and more schools embrace the power of AI, the potential for a more personal, tailored learning experience for students is growing rapidly.

Chapter 4: "Unlocking the Potential of Personalized Learning with Artificial Intelligence for K-12 Students."

The educational landscape is changing rapidly due to the emergence of artificial intelligence (AI) technologies. AI-powered technologies such as intelligent tutoring systems (Its) are making it possible for educational institutions to personalize learning experiences for K-12 students more effectively. Through intelligent tutors that can adapt and respond to individual student behaviors, teachers can provide more meaningful, individualized instruction. This paper will discuss the potential of artificial intelligence to revolutionize the K-12 learning environment for students of all ages.

Before discussing the potential of personalized learning, let us first take a look at the current state of K-12 education. Classroom instruction is typically done by a teacher lecturing with all students receiving the same material. As a result, students who struggle with understanding the material or who would benefit from a different approach to learning can find themselves falling behind with no way to catch up. Additionally, current teaching techniques often require a great deal of hands-on guidance from teachers, limiting the amount of time they can allocate to each student.

Artificial intelligence technologies provide K-12 teachers with a powerful tool for tailoring instruction and providing individualized support to each student. By utilizing Artificial Intelligence in the classroom, Educators are able to quickly identify areas of weakness within a student's performance and take action in order to improve their comprehension of the subject material. Intelligent Tutoring Systems (Its) are one of the most useful AI-powered tools available, as they enable the personalized instruction of students. These systems employ algorithms that adapt to each student's behavior and provide tutorials that are tailored to their individual needs and progress.

They are especially useful because they are able to provide immediate feedback to students as they work through guided lessons. This allows students to address their areas of difficulty and receive the assistance they need to progress in their respective studies. AI-driven applications can also suggest topics of interest that can be explored further, helping to facilitate learning and allowing students to uncover new opportunities and interests. Furthermore, AI technology is highly modular and can be applied to any subject, allowing schools to customize courses to fit the needs of their student body.

AI-driven personalized learning is also being applied to assessing student knowledge and progress, such as virtual coaches powered by AI.

Chapter 5: "Unleashing the Power of AI to Create Tailored Learning Experiences for K-12 Students".

The integration of Artificial Intelligence (AI) into the education system is a very exciting prospect, as it allows for improved learning experiences for students of all ages. AI allows for personalized and interactive learning experiences that can help to increase student engagement and increase comprehension of information. AI can also be used to develop educational materials that are tailored to the specific learning needs of each student, enabling them to have a more tailored and customized learning experience.

In the K-12 education system, AI can be used to create contextual learning experiences for students, allowing them to understand and learn topics of study from the perspective of their own unique environment. AI-based educational materials can be designed to be based on the contexts of the student, providing a more authentic learning experience that better resonates with the student. AI can also be used to provide personalized teaching assistance and feedback to students.

The use of AI in K-12 education also allows for more efficient and effective educational outcomes. AI-driven curriculum can be tailored to the unique needs of each student, allowing them to receive instruction at an optimal level of engagement and comprehension, reducing the amount of time and effort required in order to learn a topic. AI-based grading systems can also eliminate the potential for errors and grading discrepancies, providing more accurate and reliable results.

AI also has the potential to offer learning experiences that are completely self-directed. AI-driven interactive personal learning environments have been developed, which allow for the student to choose their own topics of interest and explore them with guidance from an AI system. These systems can interact with the student, both through natural language conversations and through customized information displays, to create a truly individualized learning experience that may be more engaging for the student than traditional teaching methods.

The power of AI can also be used to create effective virtual and augmented reality (VR/AR) learning experiences for students. AI-driven simulations and immersive experiences can be used to provide a realistic learning environment, allowing students to explore topics of study in a safe and engaging way. AI can also be used to create virtual textbooks and other resources that are tailored to the student's learning style and level of understanding, resulting in a more interactive and effective learning experience.

AI can be an incredibly powerful tool in the delivery of K-12 educational materials and experiences, allowing for tailored and personalized learning experiences that are tailored to the individual student's learning needs and preferences. AI-driven educational materials and experiences have the potential to revolutionize the way in which students learn and interact with their learning materials, resulting in a much more engaging and effective learning experience.

Chapter 6: "Utilizing AI to Tailor Learning Experiences for K-12 Students"

AI has become an increasingly important part of modern education, and this is especially true in the K-12 sector, where leveraging emerging technologies has the potential to greatly improve the educational experience for students. AI-enabled technologies can make instruction more personalized, interactive, and engaging, giving educators the ability to deliver tailored learning experiences for each and every student.

The incorporation of AI and machine learning into K-12 classrooms has grown immensely in recent years, with the technology enabling teachers to more precisely and personally cater to a student's individual needs. For example, AI-powered systems like natural language processing and computer vision can be used to understand student questions and provide them with more accurate and quickly delivered responses. Machine learning models can also be used to analyze large data sets of existing student performance data and generate personalized learning paths that best suit each individual student.

AI can also be used to facilitate more active and conversational learning, with chatbot systems and voice-enabled AI tools able to interact with students and provide encouragement and explanation as needed. AI can also be used to quickly identify any potential misunderstandings and adjust the level of difficulty of the material accordingly. In addition, AI-driven solutions can assess student progress, allowing teachers to allocate resources more efficiently and helping to ensure that each student is receiving the kind of support he or she needs to succeed.

That being said, AI use in K-12 classrooms isn't without its concerns and challenges. Privacy issues are particularly important in this context, and in order for AI to be used effectively, there must be rigorous security measures in place to ensure student data is kept safe. Similarly, AI solutions will need to be designed with fairness in mind to avoid any potential biases about race, gender, or any other factors that could unfairly impact a student's learning. Additionally, as with any technology, there is a risk of over-reliance on AI, and it should be used as a supplement to more traditional instructional methods, not as a replacement.

Despite these challenges, AI has immense potential to revolutionize the learning experience for K-12 students, and when used correctly, can provide tailored and personalized educational experiences for each student. AI-enabled solutions give teachers and schools the ability to adjust instruction to meet the individual needs of each student, while also offering real-time feedback and analysis of student learning progress. In the coming years, AI use in K-12 classrooms is only set to increase, and with the right combination of educational skills and technology, AI can be leveraged to transform the learning experience of K-12 students for the better.

Chapter 7: "Unleashing the Power of AI to Enhance K-12 Student Learning Experiences."

Artificial Intelligence (AI) has quickly become a buzzword in the field of education. Many experts claim that AI has the potential to revolutionize K-12 student learning experiences, and the technology is increasingly being used in schools across the world.

To better understand AI's impact on K-12 student learning experiences, it is important to have a full understanding of the concept of AI. AI refers to a computer's ability to mimic human intelligence. AI is used to automate repetitive tasks, such as differential analysis and voice recognition, as well as more complicated processes like natural language processing. In the education sector, AI has been used to assess student performance, match content to student abilities, provide personalized instruction, and more.

One way that AI can enhance K-12 student learning experiences is by personalizing content to meet individual students' learning strengths and needs. Using data such as prior performance, AI can generate custom curriculum and formats geared specifically for the student. AI can also strengthen instruction through specialized and content-specific teacher training. Educators can be provided with automated feedback and performance insights so that they can learn from best practice and tailor instruction to better engage students. AI can also suggest content from different sources and provide intuitive navigation to help students access materials they need.

Another way that AI can help to improve the K-12 learning experience is by uncovering deep learning relationships and connections. AI can identify patterns in data and suggest best learning strategies for students. Educators can be given instant feedback on the level of student engagement and performance by analyzing student data with AI algorithms. AI-powered systems can also detect new learning opportunities for students by suggesting related concepts that could expand their knowledge.

AI can play a major role in enhancing the learning experience of K-12 students by providing automation. AI technologies can automate tasks such as grading assignments and capturing student performance data, freeing up teachers to focus more on the instruction aspect of their job. Automation also can boost the accuracy of marking and assessment, reducing teacher workload and creating more time for targeted interventions and personalized instruction for students.

AI has the potential to revolutionize K-12 student learning experiences. AI can help by personalizing content to meet individual student needs, uncovering learning relationships and connections, and providing automation to reduce teacher workload. AI can be used in a range of ways, such as providing customized curriculum and instruction, generating automated feedback and insights, suggesting related content, and automating tasks such as grading and performance capture. If used correctly, AI can be a powerful tool in transforming education and helping to create more meaningful student learning experiences.

Chapter 8: "Personalizing Education with AI: Unlocking New Possibilities for K-12 Students"

The introduction of artificial intelligence (AI) into the field of education is poised to revolutionize the way K-12 students learn and achieve by providing personalized support and instruction tailored to the needs of each individual learner. On the flip side, this shift can also potentially lead to further stratification between students due to unequal access to these available technologies. In an effort to maximize the potential of AI in K-12 education, educators, administrators, and other stakeholders must ensure a fair and equitable approach to implementing these new technologies.

Technology has long been a component of K-12 education, from the earliest days of the digital revolution right up to more recent years when powerful AI solutions have been deployed. Automated systems and algorithms affect nearly every facet of student learning, from administering assessments and grading papers to individualizing instruction based on student's strengths and weaknesses. The implications of these advances carry great potential, opening up the possibility for students to receive customized education suited to their unique abilities and challenges.

The ability for AI to adapt instruction and curriculum to an individual student's needs is especially beneficial to K-12 students who face myriad learning challenges. AI can help account for different learning styles and disabilities, as well as factors such as language barriers, socio-economic backgrounds, and cultural differences. AI can also analyze and evaluate an individual student's academic progress and suggest timely interventions.

AI technologies can be used as powerful tools for supporting students' extracurricular interests and passions. AI-driven algorithms can identify scientific or artistic connections that may be useful to students like in music composition, video production, or game development. AI can also be a valuable tool in helping students of all backgrounds explore topics in history and culture, by making sophisticated research resources more accessible.

Despite the potential for real impact, the introduction of AI into K-12 education must be carried out thoughtfully and intentionally. Unequal access to these innovative technologies, or even inequitable implementation, can lead to further stratification of students and exacerbation of existing disparities. The use of AI in K-12 education must be carried out in a social justice-oriented manner, focusing particularly on grades K-5, where students' skills and abilities are still being developed. AI technologies must be used to support a student's social, emotional, and cognitive growth, while addressing systemic issues of inequality and privilege in access to certain technologies or instruction.

By understanding the potential of AI in K-12 education in both a positive and critical light, educators, administrators, and other stakeholders can work together to ensure that this new technology is integrated within an equitable framework with the aim of truly personalizing education for all students. AI-driven applications and programs should be designed with a focus on accessibility and equity to ensure that all students are afforded equitable opportunities to develop their skills, regardless of ability level or socio-economic background. When handled carefully and inclusively, AI can open up the potential for students to unleash their full potential in a personalized learning environment.

Chapter 9: "Unlocking the Potential of AI for Personalized Learning in K-12 Education."

The use of Artificial Intelligence (AI) in K-12 Education is becoming more widespread with the aim of creating an engaging and personalized learning experience for students. It is with this goal in mind that AI technologies are increasingly being used to customize learning experiences based on individual student needs. AI can draw on a range of sources to provide personalized learning experiences such as grade level, curricular materials, individual skill levels, and interest levels. By leveraging AI technology, teachers can create a dynamic learning environment which can allow students to explore a topic more deeply and develop a greater understanding and insight into the material. This paper will discuss the potential of AI in K-12 Education, how it can be used to create personalized learning experiences and the benefits it can bring.

AI technology is rapidly becoming increasingly popular in many industries, and it is no surprise that the education sector is one of them. AI can offer numerous advantages to K-12 Education, with many schools already using it to tailor their curricula to individual student needs. AI-based systems can employ a range of sources in providing personalized learning experiences such as grade level, curricular materials, individual skill levels, and interest levels. AI technology can also draw on a range of other sources, such as academic data, learning strategies, and even individual learning styles.

AI technologies can offer a range of advantages for the K-12 Education system. For instance, AI can help to create a more personalized learning experience for each student, tailored to their individual needs. AI-based systems can be used to provide personalized feedback based on the student's performance in the class. They can also be used to track a student's progress and provide personalized learning plans and strategies for improving their performance. Additionally, AI technologies can be used to analyze the data collected by teachers in order to identify areas of improvement and pinpoint the best approach for them.

AI can also be used to provide personalized reports to teachers. Using data collected from the student's progress, AI can be used to generate a report which can provide insight into the student's current performance and their areas of improvement. This can help teachers better tailor their instruction to meet each student's specific needs.

Although AI can offer many benefits to the K-12 Education system, there are some limitations to consider. For instance, AI-based systems are often expensive to implement, and their implementation and maintenance require a large amount of resources. Additionally, AI-based systems can be vulnerable to malicious attacks, which can lead to confidential data being exposed. Lastly, AI technologies are highly reliant on the quality and accuracy of the data provided to them.

AI technology has great potential for use in K-12 Education. It can be used to create a more personalized learning experience for each student, tailored to their individual needs. AI-based systems can be used to provide personalized feedback, track student progress, and generate personalized reports which can help teachers to identify areas of improvement. However, there are also some limitations to consider, such as the cost of implementation and maintenance, as well as susceptibility to malicious attacks. With careful consideration and implementation, AI technology can bring many advantages to the K-12 Education system.

Chapter 10: "Enabling Personalized Learning with Artificial Intelligence for K-12 Students."

The use of artificial intelligence (AI) in K-12 education has become increasingly widespread. AI can be used to provide personalized learning experiences to students, supporting them in their learning experience and helping them reach their educational goals. AI enables personalized education by leveraging data and advanced algorithms to develop student-specific learning plans and instructional resources, providing accurate assessments of student progress, and more. This article looks at how AI can be used to enable personalized learning in K-12 education.

AI-enabled systems use data and advanced algorithms to develop personalized learning plans and instructional resources. AI is able to process vast amounts of data about a student, including test scores, homework assignments, and other indicators of performance and personalize the learning experience accordingly. AI can use this data to quickly assess a student's strengths and weaknesses and recommend personalized activities and lesson plans to help them improve. Additionally, AI can make recommendations for educational resources tailored to meet a student's individual needs and preferences.

AI-enabled systems are able to provide highly accurate assessments of student progress. By leveraging data-driven insights and advanced algorithms, AI can provide in-depth, personalized feedback on how well students are progressing with regard to specific topics and objectives. This feedback helps teachers and parents better understand a student's progress and can be used to inform instruction and tailor instruction to the individual student's needs. AI can also monitor student performance on a granular level, alerting potential areas of concern and enabling educators to offer the support that is needed when it is needed.

AI can be used to support student engagement and motivation. AI-enabled systems can customize the learning experience to keep students engaged and encourage progress. For example, AI can be used to recommend activities or lessons that challenge the student without overwhelming them. Or AI can be used to provide positive feedback and rewards for achievement that are tailored to each student's unique interests and preferences. By using AI to customize and personalize the learning experience, educators can improve student engagement and motivation.

AI is enabling personalized learning in K-12 education. AI-enabled systems are leveraging data and advanced algorithms to develop personalized learning plans and instructional resources, provide highly accurate assessments of student progress, and support student engagement and motivation. By using AI, educators can give each student the personalized attention and instruction they need to reach their educational goals. AI is transforming K-12 education, and with it, the way students learn.

Chapter 11: "Unlocking Students' Potential with AI-Driven Personalized Learning".

Artificial intelligence (AI) is transforming the way students learn by providing personalized learning experiences tailored to each individual student. AI-driven personalized learning is the use of artificial intelligence to create an adapted learning experience for each student that considers their unique abilities, strengths, and weaknesses. By leveraging AI, educators are able to create customizable learning materials and experiences that best meet the needs of each student. This approach to learning increases student engagement and understanding, resulting in improved performance and a deeper understanding of academic content.

The use of AI-driven personalized learning has revolutionized the way students learn by catering to each student's needs, capabilities, and interests. AI-driven personalized learning solutions identify each student's strengths and weaknesses and then customize learning experiences to those individual needs. These solutions also provide tailored feedback and guidance to students as they progress, so they can identify areas of improvement and continue to strive to achieve higher levels of academic knowledge and understanding.

One way AI-driven personalized learning can be implemented is through personalized data-driven learning. Data-driven learning is the ability to get real-time insights into what is most effective for each student, allowing educators to customize their instruction and lessons to ensure maximum effectiveness and engagement. Through data-driven reports, educators can gain valuable insight into how each student is performing, as well as areas of improvement. Data-driven reporting can identify trends in test results to determine any areas that may need more attention or instruction.

Another way AI-driven personalized learning can be used is through recommendations based on the individual student. This form of personalized learning is based on tracking a student's behaviors, preferences, and abilities. It then generates individualized learning recommendations based on their unique profile. For example, if a student is interested in math and science, the AI-driven system could generate math- and science-related learning material tailored to their specific level. This approach can be invaluable in ensuring that students are consistently learning and developing skills in areas they are most interested in.

AI-driven personalized learning also offers feedback and analysis that can be used to better understand each student's performance and progress. Feedback and analysis enable educators to track each student's performance over time, as well as identify areas for improvement that can be targeted through tailored instruction or intervention instruction. This type of tailored feedback and analysis helps educators ensure that each student is fully engaged and receiving the individualized attention they need to reach their potential.

AI-driven personalized learning opens up a plethora of possibilities for how students can learn. Through personalized data-driven learning, targeted recommendations, and analysis-based feedback, educators can create a tailored learning experience for each individual student. This leads to increased student enthusiasm, engagement, and understanding, resulting in improved academic performance and a deeper knowledge base. With AI-driven personalized learning, the possibilities are limitless, and the potential is remarkable.

Chapter 12: "Leveraging AI to Enhance the Student Learning Experience: Personalizing Education for K-12 Students".

The use of Artificial Intelligence (AI) and machine learning in the field of education has been an area of increasing interest and activity in recent years. In the K-12 educational system, AI-driven technologies have the potential to offer a personalized learning experience to every student, enabling them to learn more efficiently and effectively than ever before.

Greater use of AI in K-12 education has the potential to open up new ways of learning and help improve access to quality education. AI can enhance the learning experience by automatically providing timely personalized feedback to students, based on their individual learning needs. For example, AI can analyze student history and identify patterns in subjects, evaluate candidate resources, and accurately determine effective delivery strategies.

AI can also be used to customize curriculum based on student needs. By providing a detailed analysis of each student's strengths and weaknesses, AI-driven curriculum development can help each student receive the same quality of education regardless of their background, interests, or capabilities. AI can also generate customized tests and assignments for each student, based on their performance and learning level. AI can therefore be used to meet the unique needs of each student, and ensure all learners receive effective guidance and instruction.

AI can help to automate the assessment process, enabling teachers to spend more time working one-on-one with students on their mastery of topics. AI can also provide support for problem-solving and critical thinking for developing student skills. AI-powered tools such as robotics, programming language tutors, natural language processing and computer games, can be used to develop cognitive and analytic skills outside traditional classroom settings.

AI can also help with tracking student performance over time to ensure they are making learning progress. AI-driven analysis can provide detailed insights into student performance, and provide real-time feedback on areas of improvement. This can be done by analyzing individual student progress across tests, assignments, quizzes, or projects. AI pinpoints areas where students might be struggling and can also recommend the right course of action for a particular student.

AI offers immense potential to enhance the learning experience for K-12 students. AI-powered technologies enable personalized education, providing students with personalized educational materials, its assessments tailored to individual learning levels, and real-time feedback on student performance. AI can also help to automate assessments and develop student problem-solving and critical thinking skills outside the traditional classroom. Furthermore, AI can provide useful insights into student performance for effective tracking of progress over time. Therefore, leveraging AI for K-12 education has significant potential to revolutionize the learning process and increase student engagement.

Chapter 13: "Unlocking Student Potential: Using AI to Deliver Personalized Learning in K-12 Schools"

In today's age of technology, K-12 schools are increasingly looking for ways to maximize each student's potential by delivering personalized learning. With the leveraging of Artificial Intelligence (AI), K-12 schools are now better equipped to understand the unique needs of every student. AI makes it possible for teachers to utilize data-driven insights to create lesson plans and course materials adapted to each student's individual needs.

AI allows K-12 schools to customize course materials and lesson plans according to individual student's weaknesses and strengths. By using data-driven insights, teachers can create an individualized learning plan for each student. AI can further assist in providing a more balanced distribution of educational resources between students. This is particularly important to ensure that students who are weaker in certain skills and aptitudes receive the same amount of attention as their stronger counterparts. By doing so, it is more likely that all students will unlock their potential.

AI can also help in providing personalized feedback to each student. AI, through its algorithms, is able to analyze each student's answers and provide feedback tailored specifically to them. This feedback can help the student understand their errors and learn from them. By providing feedback that is specific to the student's needs, AI can help maximize the student's learning.

AI technology is also being used to facilitate online learning. AI provides the ability to create an engaging and dynamic online learning environment that is tailored to each student's needs. By understanding the student's needs, AI can create course content which is more likely to be successful in engaging each student. This personalized approach helps to ensure that each student's individual needs are met and that the student is able to comprehend and retain the course material.

AI is also being used to assess student's progress and identify areas for improvement. AI can track a student's performance throughout the year and identify patterns of behavior that could indicate areas that need to be worked on. By utilizing AI to monitor students' performance, teachers can easily identify which topics need to be reviewed or which skills require improvement.

AI can be used for formative assessments which can detect strengths and weaknesses in each student. AI can be used to analyze student's answers to detect which areas they are struggling with or where they need to put in more effort. This can help teachers customize lesson plans and course materials to better meet the individual needs of each student.

AI can provide K-12 schools with the tools necessary to maximize the potential of every student. AI can be used to personalize lesson plans and course materials based on individual students' needs. AI can also be used to create an engaging online learning environment, assess students' progress, and identify strengths and weaknesses in every student. By taking advantage of AI's capabilities, K-12 schools will be better equipped to unlock each student's potential.

Chapter 14: "Unlocking Potential: Harnessing AI to Enhance Student Learning in K-12 Education"

The premise of Artificial Intelligence (AI) has been long-established in the media, films, and books as a revolutionary force that stands to change life as we know it. The advent of AI in the 21st century has been no different, particularly in the realm of K-12 education. AI has proven to be an invaluable technology that has the potential to revolutionize the way in which students receive their education, by focusing on personalized learning tailored to each student and enhancing their knowledge and skills while also engaging them.

Though AI's potential to improve and enhance the K-12 educational experience is undeniable, its ability to unlock the full potential of student learning in K-12 education is contingent upon certain factors. In order to unlock its potential, K-12 education needs to up its game and make use of AI that can utilize the full spectrum of its capabilities. By utilizing AI that is able to both monitor and assist students, while also taking into account different types of learning styles and learning needs, we can create a system of personalized learning that is tailored to each individual student's needs and preferences.

As AI technology advances, it opens up new possibilities for both educators and students in K-12 education. AI can be used to automate many of the school's processes, such as grading, tests, and reporting. This should not only save teachers time, but also allow them to focus on more important aspects of teaching, such as individualized instruction. AI can also be used to create more personalized learning experiences for each student, as AI algorithms can identify each student's learning style, needs, and preferences. Finally, AI technology can also help to distinguish between students who are grasping topics quickly and those who are struggling, allowing for a more efficient use of classroom resources.

For all of its potential and promise, there are still inherent risks associated with the introduction of AI into K-12 education. One of the most concerning risks is the potential for AI to create an impersonal learning environment, one where each student feels like a mere number instead of a unique individual. Furthermore, AI technology is still in its early stages and can often have inaccurate results due to unforeseen variables or unknown data. AI can also create a barrier between students and teachers, in that the teacher may feel less involved with the student's learning due to AI's automated processes.

AI technology has the potential to completely revolutionize the way in which students learn. AI can be used to help tailor the learning experience to each student's needs and preferences while also providing teachers with more accurate assessments and reports of their students' performance and progress. However, in order to truly unlock its potential, AI needs to be properly implemented and monitored to ensure students are not put at risk and that it does not create an impersonal learning environment. With the right strategies in place, AI can be an incredibly powerful force that helps K-12 students unlock their full potential.

Chapter 15: "Leveraging AI to Create a Customized Learning Experience for K-12 Students"

The potential for Artificial Intelligence (AI) in education holds a tremendous amount of promise for creating a customized learning experience for K-12 students. AI technologies are transforming the way that educators and students interact with content, assess student progress, and even predict learning outcomes. This new technology is allowing teachers to provide a personalized learning experience that is tailored to the individual student's needs.

One way AI can be used to create a customized learning experience is using adaptive learning technology. With this type of technology, a computer algorithm can be used to customize learning material and assessment strategies based on individual student data and responses. For example, the system could be designed to adjust the difficulty level of a given assignment or provide additional resources to students struggling in a specific subject area. Utilizing AI in this way can help ensure that students are provided with content that is appropriate for their level and needs, while still providing enough challenge to ensure that they stay engaged and motivated.

Another way AI can be used to create a customized learning experience is through the use of virtual tutors. AI-powered virtual tutors or chatbots can be used to provide personalized assistance to students on a range of topics. This can include helping students understand a difficult concept or providing additional guidance when working on an assignment. A virtual tutor can even use natural language processing techniques to interact with students, responding to their questions and providing additional explanations when necessary. Utilizing a chatbot or virtual tutor can be an effective way to supplement classroom instruction, enabling students to get individualized help in areas where they are struggling.

AI can also be used to create a personalized learning experience using predictive analytics. Predictive analytics allow teachers and administrators to analyze student data and identify factors that can influence student performance. This data can then be used to predict which students may struggle before they start having issues and provide them with additional support, such as additional tutoring or alternative learning methods. This approach can help ensure that students receive the level of support and attention they need in order to reach their full potential.

In addition to helping create a customized learning experience, AI can also be used to automate certain aspects of the educational process. AI-powered bots can be used to replace some tedious and time-consuming tasks typically associated with teaching, such as grading assignments or providing personalized feedback to students. Automating certain tasks can free up educators to focus more on other aspects of teaching, such as providing additional support to those students who need it most.

The potential of AI in the educational sector is quite promising. AI-based technologies have the potential to revolutionize the way that educators and students interact with learning material and assessment tools, providing an unprecedented level of personalized instruction and support. This type of personalized experience can help ensure that all students have the opportunity to reach their full potential and succeed in today's rapidly-changing education landscape.

Chapter 16: "Unlock the Potential of Personalized Learning Through AI: A Guide for K-12 Educators".

Artificial Intelligence (AI) has the potential to revolutionize how K-12 education is delivered, allowing for more personalized learning experiences for students. AI can analyze large datasets of student-specific information to create individualized learning programs for each student, offering a tailored approach to education. AI can also be used to offer real-time feedback and answers to students, as well as giving educators insight into each student's learning and cognitive abilities.

In order to unlock the full potential of using AI for education, K-12 educators must first understand how AI works. AI is a powerful tool that can be used to achieve a broad range of goals, from data mining to predictive analytics. AI works by using machine learning that "trains" computers to recognize patterns and identify trends. AI can ingest vast amounts of data, and then use algorithms to process and identify logical correlations across a variety of topics. By taking in data from a variety of sources, AI can generate valuable insights into student performance and how best to personalize learning goals.

Once K-12 educators have a clear understanding of how AI works, they can begin the process of integrating the technology into their classroom. K-12 educators will need to identify their learning objectives, as well as the desired outcomes of the AI implementation. AI can then be used to develop learning programs that employ personalized approaches based on each student's needs and abilities. AI can also be used to monitor and evaluate students' learning progress and to provide guidance and assistance where needed.

Using AI to personalize learning experiences offers numerous benefits. By tailoring instruction to each student's level, students can be provided with the right level of material to challenge, yet not overwhelm, them. Furthermore, AI can help instructors quickly gauge how much a student has retained from assigned material, and provide instantaneous feedback. AI can also offer educators an insight into each student's cognitive abilities, helping instructors build on current skills and identify areas of weakness. Finally, AI can allow for dynamic, real-time learning that adapts to each student's progress, further Engaging students and keeping them interested.

To get the most out of AI technology, K-12 educators must ensure they have the right data to support AI implementation. Data collection is essential to informing the AI system of each student's baseline understanding, providing context that the AI can use for developing personalized learning material. K-12 educators should use data points such as past grades, test results, and assessment scores to develop a clear picture of each student's current abilities and determine learning goals.

K-12 educators need to understand the ethical concerns of AI and how to ensure that data is secure and used responsibly. AI-enabled systems must help students build a sense of trust and maintain their privacy at all times. Educators should be aware of AI bias and ensure that AI-generated decisions are fair and unbiased. AI technology has tremendous potential to revolutionize K-12 education, but if not employed properly, it can end up creating more problems than solutions.

By understanding the fundamentals of AI technology, K-12 educators can unlock the potential of personalized learning through AI and create engaging learning experiences for their students. AI should be used to supplement traditional teaching methods, not replace them. AI can provide a comprehensive view of each student's learning capabilities, serving as a powerful tool to tailor instruction to individual needs. With AI, K-12 educators can ensure that each student receives the best possible education, allowing them to reach their full potential.

Chapter 17: "Optimizing Education for Every Student: Leveraging AI to Create Personalized Learning Experiences for K-12 Students."

The use of artificial intelligence (AI) in the domain of education and learning is fast becoming an important element in the educational landscape of today and beyond. AI has the potential to revolutionize the way learning takes place at the K-12 level; it can create tailored learning experiences that provide students the best possible information and skills to facilitate academic success. By leveraging AI to create personalized learning experiences, K-12 students can access content best suited to their individual needs and preferences, allowing them to learn with greater efficiency and effectiveness.

When it comes to optimizing education for every student, AI-based solutions provide a significant advantage over traditional education systems. AI-based learning systems can incorporate a variety of data, such as student profiles, classroom activities, and assessments to provide individualized instruction to every learner. This can help teachers target students' academic needs and interests more accurately, while allowing them to be more proactive in responding to these individual differences. Additionally, AI-based learning solutions can also detect learning patterns that may not be apparent to teachers and create the most effective learning plans to help improve students' academic performances.

Currently, AI technology can be used in a variety of ways to create personalized learning experiences for K-12 students, such as natural language processing, computer vision, and robotic process automation. For instance, natural language processing can be used to detect the language used by students to communicate and better match the content and material provided to them. Computer vision can be used to present content in a more interactive way to students, allowing them to have a better understanding of the educational material. In addition, robotic process automation can be used to automate certain tasks in a classroom, freeing up teacher's time for more individualized instruction.

AI technology can be used to optimize education for every student through the use of machine learning and advanced analytics. By leveraging machine learning algorithms, educational institutions can analyze massive amounts of educational data and use it to create personalized learning experiences for students. For example, machine learning approaches can be used to automatically detect individual students' strengths and weaknesses, allowing teachers to adjust the content to better fit these needs. Similarly, advanced analytics can be used to monitor every student's progress and to make data-driven decisions on how best to improve educational outcomes.

AI technology has the potential to revolutionize personalized learning experiences for K-12 students. The opportunities provided by leveraging AI to optimize education for every student should not be underestimated. AI-based learning systems can provide tailored content best suited to individual student profiles, allowing them to learn more effectively. Similarly, machine learning and advanced analytics can be used to detect student's strengths and weaknesses and to monitor their academic progress. By leveraging these powerful tools, educational institutions can create unique learning experiences that best fit the individual needs of each student.

Chapter 18: "Unleashing the Power of AI to Personalize Learning Experiences for K-12 Students".

With technology developing far faster than ever before, machine learning and artificial intelligence (AI) are becoming progressively more prevalent in today's world. This includes the field of education, where AI can be used to personalize learning experiences for K-12 students. Personalizing learning experiences can have a great impact on a student's academic progress as it helps them to better understand the material that is being presented. This article will cover the various ways AI can be used to effectively customize learning experiences to meet the needs of K-12 students.

AI is an acronym that stands for artificial intelligence. AI is a form of computer science that deals with the simulation of human intelligence by the use of computers, systems, and software. AI assists machines in performing tasks that would otherwise require human intelligence and judgment, such as recognizing speech, recognizing images, or learning from data. AI can also be used to assess and generate insights from large datasets, presenting information in an efficient and user-friendly way.

Schools are increasingly turning to AI-powered technologies to personalize learning experiences for their K-12 students, allowing them to create individualized learning plans for each student. AI technology can also be used to track student progress, track metrics, and offer feedback to teachers.

AI technology can be used to match individual student needs with appropriate learning activities and materials. AI can also be used to assess student's abilities to understand content, providing teachers with the information needed to adjust the level of content for each student. This is especially beneficial for teachers who have large classrooms, as it helps them to efficiently provide individualized instruction. AI can also be used to predict student performance and identify potential issues before they arise.

AI can also be used to provide supplemental materials and resources to students, helping them to further supplement and explore the topics they are learning. AI-powered chatbots can provide support and assistance to students 24/7, answering questions and helping them to understand material they may be struggling with. AI can also be used to detect issues and provide support, which would be particularly useful for identifying potential mental health issues among students.

AI technology holds a great potential to help personalize learning experiences for K-12 students. AI technology can match individual student needs with appropriate learning activities and materials and assess student performance and progress. AI-powered chatbots can also provide 24/7 support to students, answering their questions and helping them to understand difficult concepts. AI can also be used to provide supplemental materials and resources to help students explore topics further, as well as detect and provide support for potential mental health issues. As AI technology continues to develop, it will be increasingly used to help personalize learning experiences for K-12 students in the years to come.

Chapter 19: "Harnessing the Power of AI to Enhance Learner Outcomes in K-12 Education".

In the modern world, Artificial Intelligence (AI) has become increasingly popular and widely used in just about every sector, including education and training. As AI technology continues to be developed and evolve, its potential to help K-12 educators improve student outcomes is becoming ever more evident. Machine learning, natural language processing, and other forms of AI are already playing a significant role in K-12 classrooms, from individual student support to improving curriculum design. Here we will discuss the potential of using AI to enhance learner outcomes in K-12 education and the implications for educational reform.

AI can provide a great benefit to K-12 education by offering a more personalized approach to learning for individual students. By honing in on each student's unique learning needs, AI can offer tailored curricula and instructional materials, enabling personalized instruction to be delivered to each and every student in the classroom. AI-driven educational technology can also provide valuable real-time feedback to teachers on student progress and mastery of educational material. With access to this data, educators can more effectively assess and adjust instructional techniques to better meet the needs of each student. In addition, AI can also assist in diagnosing learning disabilities and other areas of difficulty that students may be experiencing in the classroom, so teachers can provide a more targeted and tailored approach to instruction.

AI can also be used to improve curricula design and the development of learning resources. AI, in conjunction with big data, can provide valuable insights into which educational materials are most effective and engaging for students. This can help educators make informed decisions about curriculum design and the selection of learning materials. Further, AI-driven analytics can be used to objectively assess the strengths and weaknesses of existing curricula and suggest changes or modifications that could help boost student achievement. Additionally, AI can also be used to detect and remove bias from educational materials and ensure that all students are represented accurately and fairly.

Ultimately, AI technology can help shift K-12 education from a passive model of instruction to one that is more adaptive and personalized. AI-driven educational technology can help teachers better understand each student's individual learning needs, so they can provide tailored instruction that is designed to achieve the highest possible student outcomes. AI also has the potential to reduce potential sources of bias in instructional materials and curricula, and make the development and selection of learning resources quicker and more cost-effective. With AI, K-12 educators can provide a more equitable and engaging learning environment for all students and thus help to improve student outcomes.

Chapter 20: "Leveraging AI to Enhance Student Learning and Engagement in the Classroom".

The use of artificial intelligence (AI) in the classroom is becoming increasingly commonplace as educators look to leverage this powerful technology to improve student learning and engagement. AI has the potential to revolutionize the way in which students learn, interact, collaborate, and find success in their learning environment. Using AI tools and resources, student engagement can be improved significantly while also enhancing student performance. This article will explore some ways in which AI can improve student learning and engagement in the classroom.

One of the primary ways in which AI can be used to improve student learning and engagement is through the use of intelligent personal assistants. These assistants can be used to provide personalized learning experiences for individual students, which can help them stay focused and motivated during the class. Intelligent personal assistants can also be programmed to monitor student progress and provide feedback on their work. This feedback can then be used to encourage students and help them gain further insight into the material being taught.

Another avenue for leveraging AI to improve student learning and engagement is to integrate AI-based tools and resources into lessons and activities. For instance, AI can be used to generate personalized activities based on student preferences and interests, enabling students to engage in learning activities more tailored to their individual needs. Additionally, AI can be used to create individualized learning paths, which can provide students with differentiated instruction that best meets their individual needs. By providing personalized learning experiences, AI can help motivate students and encourage them to stay engaged and make progress in their courses.

AI can also be used to facilitate collaboration among students, enabling them to work together more effectively and explore new ideas. For example, AI can be used to create virtual classrooms, allowing students to access a range of collaboration tools such as discussion boards and chatbots. These collaboration tools can help generate new insights and allow students to better engage with one another, which can improve student engagement and learning on the whole.

AI can help educators assess student work more accurately and efficiently, allowing them to identify areas in which individual students may need additional support or instruction. AI-based assessment tools can be used to analyze student work quickly and accurately, giving educators a better understanding of student progress and enabling them to tailor instruction to meet individual student needs. This assists in ensuring that students stay on track and understand the material they are being taught.

As demonstrated, AI can be a powerful tool for enhancing student learning and engagement in the classroom. By leveraging AI-based tools and resources, students can be provided with personalized learning experiences, engage in meaningful collaborations with their peers, and receive accurate and timely assessments of their work. This technology has great potential to revolutionize the way students learn and interact in the classroom, creating a more engaging, stimulating, and successful learning environment for all.

Chapter 21: "Unleashing the Power of AI to Personalize Learning for K-12 Students".

In recent years, Artificial Intelligence (AI) has become increasingly popular as a tool for personalizing learning for K-12 students. AI can provide personalized learning experiences that are tailored to the individual learning needs of each student. AI has the potential to increase engagement in the classroom, improve student outcomes, and create meaningful learning experiences. Furthermore, AI can help teachers to create personalized learning plans, recommend resources, and provide real-time feedback.

AI can be used to personalize learning for K-12 students by adapting the curriculum to each student's individual needs, preferences, and interests. AI can provide tailored content and lessons for each student by utilizing data analysis and machine learning. AI can go beyond traditional learning models to provide an interactive and engaging learning experience. AI can take into account each student's learning style, habits, and interests and use this data to create personalized learning experiences.

AI can also help teachers to create personalized learning plans for their students. AI can assist teachers in selecting content, creating schedules, and assigning tasks. AI can provide real-time feedback to both teachers and students, and can detect patterns and trends in student behavior. This can help teachers to determine which instructional strategies are most effective for a particular group of students. AI can also assist teachers in creating individualized plans for each student, taking into account their individual needs and capabilities.

AI can provide personalized learning experiences for K-12 students by recommending educational resources that are tailored to their individual needs. AI can use data analysis and machine learning to recommend resources to students based on their individual interests and capabilities. With AI, students can explore and discover their interests and develop their skills in personalized and targeted ways. AI can also provide personalized tutoring services to students who need extra assistance.

AI can help to create meaningful learning experiences for K-12 students. AI can target each student's interests and preferences to create engaging learning experiences. AI can provide interactive simulations, virtual reality experiences, and adaptive learning systems that can help students to engage more deeply with the subject. AI can also allow teachers to customize their instruction based on the individual needs of their students, and provide targeted feedback to help guide students along the way.

AI can provide a wide range of personalized learning experiences for K-12 students. AI can help teachers to develop targeted curricula, create personalized learning plans, recommend educational resources, and provide real-time feedback. With the help of AI, teachers can create engaging learning experiences that are tailored to each student's individual needs. AI can help to create meaningful learning experiences that can help K-12 students to reach their full potential.

Chapter 22: "Unlocking New Possibilities: Using AI to Tailor Learning for K-12 Students"

Artificial Intelligence (AI) has rapidly become a part of our everyday lives, transforming how we think, talk, and interact with technology. AI has also made an impact on the education sector, particularly K-12, enabling an unprecedented level of customized and personalized learning for each student.

AI provides new ways for students to learn by using a broad array of data to tailor content and instruction to individual needs. By allowing educators to automatically customize educational materials to fit their students, AI can make learning more efficient, effective, and enjoyable. AI can also identify and close learning gaps more quickly than traditional methods, allowing students to reach their academic and developmental goals more quickly.

The potential of AI-assisted learning is especially evident in K-12 education. By leveraging its expansive data capabilities, AI can provide tailored instruction to each of its students, and create adaptive content and personalized experiences. This allows teachers and educators to quickly understand each student's individual strengths and weaknesses, providing targeted materials and instruction that are tailored to their unique needs.

AI also helps provide a more consistent learning experience across all students. Instead of relying on a single expert to provide instruction, AI can analyze data from a variety of sources and outline the best learning paths for each student. By forming an on the whole picture of the skills each student needs to learn, AI can provide each student with the support they need to progress and make progress faster.

AI-assisted learning can also provide insight to teachers, allowing them to quickly spot patterns in their students' behavior. For instance,

AI can detect when a student has a problem understanding a particular concept, and help teachers adjust their methods accordingly. AI can even detect when students are getting distracted and help teachers provide the right form of guidance to keep students focused. By giving educators more insights, AI helps them not only teach better, but also better understand their students, empowering them to provide better instruction and guidance.

AI can help reduce costs for educational institutions by providing a more efficient way to assess learning progress. AI can automate large portions of data analysis, allowing educators to quickly assess student progress and identify issues. By leveraging AI-driven assessment tools, educators can ensure that no student falls behind, and that they can identify any potential issues quickly and easily.

AI is transforming the way we think about K-12 education. With its powerful analysis capabilities, AI is enabling an unprecedented level of personalized learning experiences, increasing the efficiency of assessments, and providing valuable insight to teachers. AI is unlocking an exciting and new level of possibilities for K-12 students to reach their full potential, helping them achieve more in their educational pursuits.

Chapter 23: "Constructing a Personalized Learning Experience with AI in K-12 Education"

The use of artificial intelligence (AI) in K-12 education is a relatively new and increasingly important field of study. AI has the potential to revolutionize education by providing personalized learning experiences for all students. This technology has the power to identify patterns in student data, tailor instruction to individual needs, and facilitate improved instructional practices. This potential has sparked interest in exploring ways to construct personalized learning experiences with AI in K-12 education.

Creating personalized learning experiences with AI requires a comprehensive approach to establishing a technology architecture and developing tools that enable AI-enhanced instruction. First, it is important to establish a data-driven learning system that is capable of gathering data from various sources to better target lesson planning and delivery. This includes data such as student performance, course progress, attendance, responses to assignments and assessments, and so on. This data can be used to gain insights into each student's strengths and weaknesses, identify learning gaps, and customize learning plans and objectives. For example, AI systems could use data to target assessments and prescribe more effective instructional strategies, recommend resources that fit individual students' abilities or needs, and track learning progress so that instruction can be tailored to students' specific abilities.

Second, it is important to create AI tools which support instructional decisions and provide value to the learning environment. This can include tools such as natural language processing to support conversations between instructors and students and automated grading of essay-style assessments. AI tools can also be used to provide students with feedback and guidance in real-time while studying, provide personalized learning paths, and recommend resources to support learning objectives. Such AI tools can also be designed to engage with students outside the classroom. For instance, AI might use data to plan and adjust lesson content, recognize student engagement, and offer advice and assistance to students who are struggling with a particular subject.

Finally, it is important to equip instructors with the knowledge and tools to effectively incorporate AI into their courses. This includes using data to inform instruction, understanding the limitations of AI-based predictions and recommendations, and developing principles and best practices for using AI in teaching. Instructors should also have the opportunity to build and customize AI-enhanced learning strategies if desired, and receive training or ongoing support from AI developers.

The idea of constructing personalized learning experiences with AI in K-12 education presents exciting possibilities for the future of education. By creating data-driven learning systems and developing AI tools to support instructional decisions, education can be more personalized and engaging. By equipping instructors with the necessary knowledge and tools to effectively incorporate AI into their courses, AI can be used to create effective learning experiences for all students. AI can also provide a more comprehensive and timely assessment of student learning progress and engagement. Ultimately, developing personalized learning experiences with AI in K-12 education can help create a more equitable and exciting educational experience for all students.

Chapter 24: "Unlocking the Potential of AI to Enhance Learning Experiences in K-12 Education"

Artificial Intelligence (AI) has the potential to significantly enhance learning experiences in K-12 education. Artificial Intelligence (AI) technology can be used to create interactive, personalized learning experiences tailored to each student's individual needs. AI can also automate tedious administrative tasks, such as grading exams, providing feedback, and assigning homework. Moreover, AI can be used to provide predictive analysis, allowing teachers and administrators to identify and address underlying issues that may be hindering a student's academic progress.

In order to unlock the potential of AI, educational institutions must begin by developing the necessary infrastructure. This includes creating custom AI algorithms, designing physical hardware, and implementing AI software. All of these components must be properly integrated into the existing educational systems and processes. Many schools may lack the resources necessary to build a comprehensive AI system from scratch, so it is important to consider partnering with existing technology companies that specialize in AI for education.

Once the necessary infrastructure is in place, K-12 schools can begin to explore the potential of AI to enhance learning experiences in numerous ways. For example, AI can be used to customize each student's learning/ teaching environment based on their individual needs. AI algorithms can track a student's progress, provide personalized feedback, and adjust curricula and teaching methods accordingly. AI can also automate administrative tasks such as reviewing students' homework, grading exams, and tracking attendance. AI can also provide predictive analytics to identify trends in data and provide insights into why students are struggling.

AI technology has the potential to improve educational outcomes and provide students with greater access to learning materials. AI algorithms can be used to detect and solve potential problems in curricula before they become apparent and to make sure that the presented information is always up-to-date. AI can also facilitate more accurate access to distance learning, either through the use of virtual classrooms or online portals. AI can be used to ensure that each student has access to the same educational materials even when they are located in different parts of the world.

AI can play an important role in helping teachers to identify at-risk students. AI can analyze data from multiple sources, such as student performance, attendance records, and test scores. AI can also help identify potential issues such as anxiety, depression, or difficulty concentrating related to a student's home environment. AI can also help teachers identify students who may be struggling with a specific subject area, allowing them to provide more targeted instruction and assistance.

AI has the potential to revolutionize the way in which schools measure and assess student progress. AI technology can be used to track and analyze data from all assignments, exams, and coursework over time. AI can use this information to provide teachers with valuable insights into the effectiveness of their instruction. AI can also be used to recommend personalized teaching methods for each student, helping to ensure that they are receiving the best possible education.

AI technology has the potential to significantly improve learning experiences in K-12 education. AI can be used to customize each student's learning/teaching environment, automate administrative tasks, and provide predictive analytics. AI can also be used to improve educational outcomes, give students greater access to learning materials, identify at-risk students, and measure and assess student progress. In order to unlock this potential, K-12 schools must first develop an appropriate AI infrastructure, before exploring the various ways in which AI can be leveraged to enhance learning experiences.

Chapter 25: "Tailoring Education with AI: Unlocking Individualized Learning Experiences for K-12 Students."

Education represents a growing industry in the world, to unlock each student's potential. With AI, educational systems are leveraging technology to ensure all students have the highest quality education experience. Currently, AI-based solutions are being used to tailor an individualized learning experience by providing personalization for each student's learning pace and style.

AI-based educational solutions are being developed to provide students with tools to improve their learning experiences. For example, AI-based algorithms are being used to analyze student data to identify areas where students may need extra help. This information can then be used to customize learning materials to better meet each student's needs, allowing them to master concepts more quickly and efficiently. Additionally, AI-based applications are being used to develop personalized and individualized learning approaches, providing interactive and game-based learning experiences that are more engaging and enjoyable for students.

Another way in which AI is contributing to K-12 education is in the use of chatbots. Chatbots are AI-based virtual assistants that are used to answer student questions and provide personalized assistance. This kind of technology is particularly helpful in cases where there are no available teachers or human intervention available. Chatbots can provide students with the information they need in an intuitive and interactive way.

AI is also being used to deliver highly customizable digital assessments. Such assessments are capable of dynamically altering questions to suit each student's level of understanding. This means that the same exam can be used to assess different students and their performance can be tracked over time. This enables educators to gain a better understanding of each student's level of knowledge and areas which require further attention.

One of the main benefits of AI-based technologies in K-12 education is that they are able to eliminate many of the time-consuming and tedious tasks involved in managing large classrooms. AI-enabled automation can be used to manage large groups of students with minimal human intervention, allowing teachers to focus more of their time and energy on providing quality education to their students. Additionally, AI-based applications can facilitate collaborative learning, as students can connect with each other and share learning materials.

AI can also be used to deliver feedback to students in a more timely and tailored manner. This means that students are able to receive real-time feedback on their performance in class and can adjust their own learning strategies accordingly. This allows for a more dynamic learning experience and helps students master concepts faster and more effectively.

AI presents an exciting opportunity to create personalized and individualized learning experiences for K-12 students. AI-based solutions provide students with tools to identify areas of need more effectively, as well as tailor-made educational experiences that are more engaging and enjoyable. AI also has the potential to better analyze student data and provide feedback quicker and more accurately, leading to a more comprehensive learning process. By utilizing AI-based technologies, K-12 education can become much more tailored and effective, allowing students to unlock their full potential.

Chapter 26: "Elevating Education: Leveraging AI to Transform K-12 Learning Experiences."

The success of K-12 education has long been recognized as an important cornerstone in the development of a future-ready workforce and individuals who are well-prepared to contribute to the greater good of society. Schools all over the world are now taking an increasingly stronger stance on the importance of technology-driven, data-driven, and AI-driven services to help improve students' educational experiences. While educational institutions of all varieties have traditionally relied on technology and automation to help support their operations, the integration of AI is rapidly transforming more and more aspects of the K-12 experience with the aim of improving outcomes.

At its core, AI refers to technologies that are used to make decisions or automate processes that would otherwise be carried out by humans. In the case of K-12 education, this corporate refers to the use of Artificial Intelligence (AI) tools to assist with various aspects of the educational process, including teaching, learning, assessment, and the management of various aspects of the schools themselves. AI solutions are already being utilized in the K-12 environment, offering a range of services, such as automated grading, personalized learning programs, and cloud-based solutions to improve the on the whole experience of K-12 schools and educators.

AI presents an incredible opportunity for K-12 educators and administrators to leverage data and technology to elevate the educational experience. AI-driven solutions, such as automated grading, can reduce the tutor's workload and time spent on administrative tasks and other non-teaching responsibilities. AI-driven solutions can also provide students with personalized learning experiences that are tailored to their individual needs and goals. This approach can potentially increase engagement, allow students to stay on track, and help foster independent learning and problem-solving skills. AI's predictive capabilities can help administrations better understand which approaches and resources to deploy to optimize learning outcomes. In addition, AI can also be used to help with various administrative tasks, such as managing attendance records, generating reports, and helping to identify any potential achievement or skill gaps.

AI-driven solutions can also help to facilitate collaboration and sharing of both learning materials and best practices. AI-based cloud storage solutions can be used to improve communication between teachers and students, as well as with school administrators. This can lead to a better on the whole operation and performance of the school. Additionally, AI-powered recommendations can be utilized to help educators discover new methods of teaching and assessment that can potentially help improve learning outcomes and engagement.

The integration of AI into K-12 education has undeniably been a positive step forward in many ways. That said, there are still a number of challenges associated with utilizing AI in the K-12 environment that need to be addressed. First and foremost, prior to implementation of AI, there must be a comprehensive understanding and assessment of data security risks. Additionally, standards of training and development need to be established to ensure that educators have the necessary training and resources to harness the full potential of AI-driven services. Finally, organizations need to ensure that AI solutions take into account the diverse needs of different schools and students, while also being mindful of fairness and equity when it comes to access and use of technology, data, and services.

The use of AI in K-12 education presents an incredible opportunity for both students and educators alike. With the right approaches and the necessary precautions, K-12 schools have the potential to transform their teaching and learning experiences while simultaneously preparing students for the future. The integration of AI into K-12 education has the potential to open up an entirely new world of teaching and learning, paving the way for a future where the education experience is both innovative and successful.

Chapter 27: "Unlocking the Potential of AI-Powered Personalized Learning for K-12 Students"

The potential of AI-powered personalized learning for K-12 students is immense. By leveraging the advantages of AI, teachers and educators can provide personalized instruction tailored to each student, enabling them to reach their full potential. AI-powered personalized learning can be a major advantage for K-12 students. It can help them develop the skills and competencies required to succeed in the 21st century. Additionally, it can provide them with scaffolded instruction, actionable feedback, and personalized guidance that can improve learning outcomes and maximize learning potential.

The increasing availability of data and machine learning algorithms is making it possible to use AI-based personalized learning solutions in K-12 classrooms. This technology can analyze student data and present recommendations for action in real-time. For example, it can identify topics that individual students are struggling with and provide guidance on how to remedy them. In addition, it can track and observe student progress over time. With this data, teachers can make informed decisions about curriculum, instruction, and assessment tailored to individual student needs.

AI-based personalized learning can also provide personalized instruction to students at different grade levels and across various subject areas. For example, it can help teachers adapt instructional materials to fit student learning styles and preferences. It can also assist teachers in creating individualized learning plans for each student, allowing them to set personalized goals and track their progress. AI-based personalized learning can also enable teachers to target interventions to students who require additional support.

By offering personalized instruction, AI-powered personalized learning can also use data to inform decision-making related to teaching. For instance, prediction models can provide predictions about student performance in certain courses or subject areas. This information can aid in curriculum design, lesson planning, and assessment creation. AI can also inform pedagogy, enabling teachers to develop targeted instructional strategies tailored to meet the unique needs of each student.

AI-powered personalized learning can also help improve student engagement and motivation. AI-based technology can analyze student data to uncover areas of interest and create targeted lessons or activities tailored to individual student needs. This will help keep students interested and motivated to learn and succeed. Additionally, AI can be used to support and vocalize student emergent ideas, allowing the teacher and peers to better understand and contribute to the ideas presented.

AI-based personalized learning can create a more equitable learning environment. By providing personalized instruction to each student tailored to their individual needs, AI-powered personalized learning can help close the achievement gap among different student populations. Additionally, AI can be used to match resources and opportunities with individual student needs. This technology can help ensure that each student is receiving the support they need to reach their full potential regardless of their backgrounds or circumstances.

The potential of AI-powered personalized learning for K-12 students is enormous. By leveraging the available data and machine learning algorithms, teachers and educators can provide personalized instruction tailored to individual student needs, helping them reach their full potential. AI-based personalized learning can also help improve student engagement, motivation, and equity in the classroom. As the use of AI-powered personalized learning continues to expand, its potential to improve student learning outcomes will continue to grow.

Chapter 28: "Leveraging AI to Create Engaging and Personalized Learning Experiences for K-12 Students"

Technology has seen an incredible advancement in the last few decades, and with it has come great opportunities for change in the educational system. Artificial Intelligence (AI) is one such technology that has the potential to revolutionize the way students learn, interact and engage with educational materials.

AI can be used to create highly personalized and engaging learning experiences for K-12 students. AI-driven learning technologies are rapidly becoming accepted as a way of creating an immersive and individualized experience for K-12 students. AI-driven education provides significant value in resulting in higher engagement rates and improved performance indicators.

Personalization plays an important role in AI giving context to the student's abilities, desires and preferences, enabling materials to be tailored to the individual. AI-driven technologies can analyze an individual's traits and generate a custom experience to suit their learning style and preferences. AI-powered technologies use supervised learning techniques to analyze the student's previous activities and data points to create an AI-driven individualized experience. This enables stepwise learning, allowing complexity and difficulty level to be chosen according to the student's abilities.

By leveraging AI, K-12 students are exposed to an interactive and customized learning experience. AI-driven technologies offer adaptive learning platforms that can be used to customize the learning process in order to better suit the student's individual learning needs. This includes features such as personalized reading materials, customizable homework assignments, curated lesson plans, and customized assessments. Adaptive learning technologies enable teachers to measure student performance and adjust the difficulty and depth of lessons according to the student's ability and comprehension level. This ensures that the student is learning at an appropriate pace and that there is a low risk of students falling through the cracks.

Apart from personalized learning experiences, AI-driven technologies can also be used to create interactive and engaging learning experiences for K-12 students. AI-driven technologies can use natural language processing (NLP) to generate engaging and interactive virtual learning materials tailored to the student's interests and preferences. AI-driven technologies can also be used to create augmented reality applications such as virtual field trips or interactive 3D simulations to promote real-world learning experiences. AI-driven technologies enable students to directly engage with the content being taught, encouraging greater learning outcomes.

AI-driven technologies, such as machine learning algorithms, can also be used to analyze student interactions with learning materials in order to provide real-time feedback. The AI-driven technology can analyze the student interactions and provide targeted advice or hints that guide the student in the right direction. This real-time feedback enables the student to receive feedback on their learning progress and helps to inform the teacher on areas of improvement or difficulty.

AI-driven educational technologies offer a personalized and engaging learning experience for K-12 students. AI-driven technologies can be used to create a personalized learning experience for K-12 students by analyzing their data points, providing interactive and engaging learning materials, and analyzing student interactions and providing real-time feedback to guide further progression. AI-driven technologies will help to ensure greater student engagement and improved learning outcomes.

Chapter 29: "Unlocking the Potential of AI to Create Customized Learning Experiences for K-12 Students."

The advent of Artificial Intelligence (AI) has revolutionized the way educators around the world are thinking about teaching and learning in the 21st century. AI is being used to create personalized learning experiences for K-12 students in courses of all disciplines, from mathematics to social studies and beyond.

AI is helping streamline personalized learning within K-12 classrooms, making it easier and more efficient for teachers to customize instruction to each individual student's needs. With AI, teachers can identify their students' strengths and weaknesses more accurately, providing the most appropriate and effective learning paths for students to follow. AI also provides insights into the types of materials that will engage students and keep them interested in learning. AI learning systems are being used to quickly identify gaps in student knowledge and to recommend appropriate supplemental reading material or activities to plug those gaps.

To create tailored learning experiences for K-12 students, AI systems also take into account out-of-class considerations, such as socio-economic factors, cultural diversity, or language or literacy proficiency. For example, AI solutions are capable of assessing whether a student's learning environment is in sync with that student's performance and can adjust instruction accordingly. AI systems can also accommodate different learning styles and preferences, as well as various levels of instructional complexity.

AI-based solutions are designed to provide a personalized learning experience that continues outside the classroom, enabling students to continue to grow and learn from the comfort of their own homes. AI-based solutions may include adaptive learning courses, interactive tutorials, and personalized recommendations for online supplemental resources. With this type of learning platform, students can learn at their own pace, as AI provides feedback and guidance on the material to help them stay on track.

AI technology can be used to help teachers develop more engaging and effective lesson plans. AI solutions can be used to analyze data collected from previous lessons, such as which materials resonated the most with students and which teaching techniques worked the best. This analysis can help teachers better plan their curriculum and lesson delivery so that students are consistently engaged and learn the material more effectively.

The potential of AI to create customized learning experiences for K-12 students is vast. As AI-based solutions continue to evolve and become more user-friendly, they will be positioned to make an even bigger impact in the classroom, helping educators everywhere to ensure their students are receiving the best instruction and learning opportunities possible.

Chapter 30: "Unlocking the Potential of Artificial Intelligence in the Classroom to Enhance Student Learning."

In recent years, there has been a dramatic increase in the use of Artificial Intelligence (AI) in the classroom. AI is a branch of computer science involved with creating intelligent machines that can think and work autonomously. AI has the potential to change the way students learn by literally bringing machines to the classroom. By leveraging AI, teachers can create highly interactive and engaging learning experiences that can improve student understanding and retention.

The use of AI in the classroom has the potential to unlock the full range of student learning opportunities. AI can be employed to provide students with tailored learning experiences that are tailored to their particular needs. By tailoring the curriculum to individual students, teachers can ensure that no student is left behind or falls behind. AI can also be used to provide personalized feedback on student performance and progress. This personalized feedback can highlight areas for students to focus on and also encourage students to explore more in-depth areas of the curricula.

AI can also be used to provide students with more immersive learning experiences. For example, virtual reality technology can be used to create environments where students can explore different scenarios and problem solve in real time. Additionally, AI can be used to create interactive simulations in the classroom which allow students to explore concepts more easily. AI can be used to monitor the activities of the students and provide them with feedback in real time.

AI can be used to provide students with virtual learning environments. These virtual learning environments can be tailored to meet the individual objectives and interests of each student. For example, AI can be used to create virtualized classrooms, interactive 3D models, virtual gaming platforms, and custom-made tools for problem-solving. These technologies can enable students to interact with their peers in an environment that allows them to think and respond to problems in real time.

AI can also be used to create assessment tools and evaluation systems. These systems can be used to track the progress of students and measure their engagement and understanding of a lesson. By using AI, teachers can easily identify areas of the curriculum where students need more support and can provide additional instruction as needed. AI can also be used to generate report cards and give personalized recommendations to students based on their performance.

The potential of AI in the classroom is immense and can be used to enhance student learning in a variety of ways. AI can provide personalized learning experiences, create immersive learning environments, enable virtual learning, and create assessment tools and evaluation systems. With these features, AI can help teachers unlock the full learning potential of their students.

Don't miss out!

Visit the website below and you can sign up to receive emails whenever Adam Smith publishes a new book. There's no charge and no obligation.

https://books2read.com/r/B-A-OSAW-UZTJC

BOOKS 2 READ

Connecting independent readers to independent writers.

Also by Adam Smith

AI in K-12 Education

Intelligent Machines in the Classroom: Unlocking the Potential of AI in K12 Education

Making Sense of AI in K12 Education: A Guide for Teachers, Administrators, and Parents

The Future of Learning: Artificial Intelligence in K12 Education

Towards an AI-Infused Revolution in K12 Education

Unleashing AI in the Classroom: Strategies for Implementing Intelligent Technologies in K-12 Education

Unleashing the Potential of Artificial Intelligence in K-12 Education: Reimagining How Learning Happens

Breaking Down Bad Habits

Breaking Down Bad Habits: How to Overcome Self-Defeating Behaviors and Achieve Success

Standalone

Brain Dead: When It Comes To Improving Mental Health, What The Hell Are We Waiting For?

40 Things Intelligent People Do Daily

The Beginner's Guide to Quantum Computing & Mechanics
Open Source AI

Watch for more at https://books2read.com/adamsmith.

About the Author

Adam Smith is a native North Texas Entrepreneur, AI educational expert, and educator who graduated from Embry Riddle University with a Bachelor of Science in Aerospace Studies. In 2007 he co-founded TeacherTube.com, an online education platform community that provides an educationally focused, safe venue for teachers, schools, and home learners. Under his leadership, in September of 2017, a publicly traded company, Salem Media Group, acquired TeacherTube.

After the acquisition, Adam continued his passion for technology and education by helping schools and start-ups to large corporations with digital consulting.

Read more at https://books2read.com/adamsmith.

A. SMITH

MEDIA

Publishing Division | Texas

About the Publisher

A. Smith Media is a fully integrated digital media and distribution company specializing in producing and marketing television, film, home entertainment, music, and interactive games. A. Smith Media has been at the forefront of the commercial growth of Digital Distribution and Internet Video on Demand services through its pioneering efforts in web TV.

www.ingramcontent.com/pod-product-compliance
Lightning Source LLC
LaVergne TN
LVHW022314200926
848481LV00004B/1331

* 9 7 9 8 2 2 3 8 6 5 7 8 0 *